Integrated Science

Science

for the **Caribbean**

Gene Samuel

Advisors:
Shameem Narine, Nadine Victor-Ayers,
Ishaq Mohammed, Sheldon Rivas

Workbook 1

updated

Collins

HarperCollins*Publishers* Ltd
The News Building
1 London Bridge Street
London SE1 9GF

HarperCollins*Publishers*
Macken House, 39/40
Mayor Street Upper,
Dublin 1, D01 C9W8, Ireland

Updated edition 2017

10 9 8

This book is produced from independently certified FSC™ paper to ensure responsible forest management.

For more information visit: www.harpercollins.co.uk/green

ISBN 978-0-00-826305-8

www.collins.co.uk/caribbeanschools

A catalogue record for this book is available from the British Library.

Typeset by QBS Learning
Printed and Bound in India by Replika Press Pvt. Ltd.

Author: Gene Samuel
Advisors: Shameem Narine, Nadine Victor-Ayers, Ishaq Mohammed, Sheldon Rivas
Illustrators: QBS Learning
Publisher: Elaine Higgleton
Commissioning Editor: Tom Hardy
Editor: Julianna Dunn
Project Manager: Alissa McWhinnie, QBS Learning

Proofreader: Helen Bleck
Cover Design: Gordon MacGilp
Production: Rachel Weaver

Contents

1.1–1.2 Science and technology

1 What is science? _____

_____

_____

_____

[2]

2 The two areas into which the many branches of science are grouped are natural

sciences and _____ sciences.

[1]

3 Choose which area of study matches each branch of science. Put A, B, C, D, E, F,
G, H, I or J in the boxes provided in the right-hand column.

	BRANCH OF SCIENCE		AREA BEING STUDIED	
A	Meteorology		Healing	
B	Chemistry		Animals	
C	Geology		Living things	
D	Medicine		Atmosphere	
E	Zoology		Objects beyond earth	
F	Physics		Behaviour of matter	
G	Biology		Number, quantity and shape and space	
H	Botany		Behaviour of the composition of matter	
I	Mathematics		Structures of the earth	
J	Astronomy		Plants	

[5]

4 What is technology? _____

_____

_____

_____

[2]

5 Complete the table below by identifying SIX inventions.

Describe some of the advantages and disadvantages of each one.

INVENTION	ADVANTAGES	DISADVANTAGES

[12]

6 Imagine you are being funded to invent something that will be useful in hospitals. Give its

a) i) name _____

[1]

ii) use _____

_____

[2]

iii) advantages _____

_____

[2]

iv) disadvantages _____

_____

[2]

b) Provide a diagram or illustration of your invention.

[2]

7 Choose TWO scientists you know about and state what made each of them famous.

_____

_____

_____

_____

[4]

8 Give the meaning of these key terms.

a) Observation _____

b) Experiment _____

c) Application _____

[3]

1.3 Scientific skills and methods

1 Why is it necessary for scientists to be organized? _____

_____

_____

[2]

2 Indicate whether each of the following is TRUE or FALSE.

a) The main products of science are lab skills and data. _____

b) Scientists always try to search for answers to their own questions. _____

c) Science is a process of inquiry. _____

d) Scepticism is very important to science. _____

e) One who is curious may never be a good scientist. _____

f) A good scientist is orderly in work and disciplined in thought. _____

g) Modern science emerged about 1950. _____

h) At present psychology is seen only as a social science. _____

i) Science is a system of beliefs. _____

j) In time, science will solve all the problems of society. _____

[10]

3. Use the clues to complete this crossword puzzle on science skills.

Across

2. State expected outcomes based on experience
8. Use instruments to acquire information
9. Control different factors that might affect test results
10. Group objects according to certain characteristics
11. Carry out a set of activities in an attempt to achieve a goal
12. Translate information into tables, diagrams, words for it to be easily understood

Down

1. Collect information via the senses
2. Formulate an orderly set of events which may lead to achieving a goal
3. Deduce or conclude
4. Explain or _____ numerical information
5. Make statements in such a way that they can be verified
6. Gather all ideas on paper
7. Gather numerical information or collect _____

[13]

1.4 Writing an experiment report

1 Why is it necessary for scientists to write a detailed report of their experiments?

_____

_____

[2]

2 The following are parts from various lab reports. Identify under which section of the report each should be written.

	PART OF LAB REPORT	SECTION OF LAB REPORT
a)	The flame was green because a reaction had occurred.	
b)	All the rods were of the same thickness.	
c)	The solution was heated over a Bunsen flame.	
d)	It was found that none of the metals could rust.	
e)	To examine the activity of cells under a microscope.	
f)	Acid and alkali reactions.	

[6]

1.5–1.6 Making and labelling scientific drawings

1 Examine the diagram of the eye below. List FOUR things which are incorrect about it for a scientific diagram.

a) _____

_____

b) _____

_____

c) _____

_____

d) _____

_____

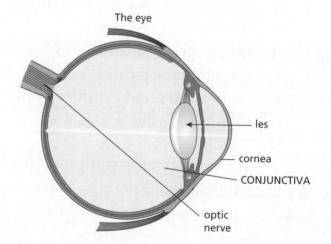

The eye

les

cornea

CONJUNCTIVA

optic nerve

[4]

2 Explain the meaning of the following terms.

a) Annotated _____

_____

_____

b) Magnification _____

_____

_____

c) Specimen _____

_____

_____

[3]

1.7 Scientific apparatus

1 Draw the apparatus named in each box below.

Conical flask	Test tube	Beaker

[3]

2 Name the apparatus in each box below.

a)

_____

b)

_____

c)

_____

[3]

3 Which type of flame is shown on each burner below?

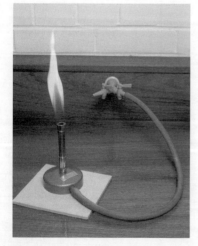

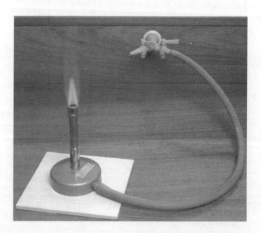

a) _____

_____

b) _____

_____

[2]

Circle the correct answer in questions 4–5.

4 During an experiment, some chemical is collected in a beaker. Which apparatus could best be used to replace the beaker?

a) Measuring cylinder   b) Round bottomed flask

c) Flat bottomed flask   d) Conical flask

5 Which one of the following would NOT be used over a flame?

a) Test tube   b) Evaporating dish   c) Beaker   d) Pipette

[2]

6 Use the clues below to complete the crossword puzzle on lab apparatus.

Across

4. For measuring accurately a specific volume of liquid (e.g. 50 cm cubed or 25 cm cubed)

6. _____ bottomed flask for preparation of gases if the process requires heating

8. _____ burner to provide a flame for heating

9. For heating solids over a flame

10. For containing chemicals or collecting liquids

Down

1. _____ bottomed flask for preparation of gases if no heating is required

2. _____ stand for supporting apparatus during heating

3. For containing or heating small amounts of substances

5. Filter _____ for separating an insoluble solid from a liquid with the help of filter paper

7. Measuring _____ for measuring very accurately the volume of liquids

[10]

11

1.8–1.9   Safety in the school laboratory

Circle the correct answer in questions 1–4.

1 Glass tubing should be removed from rubber stoppers

   a) with soapy water

   b) with extreme caution

   c) only when the glass is broken

   d) with water and a rag.

2 Hold bottles with your hand over the label while pouring to

   a) protect the label

   b) prevent contamination

   c) avoid others identifying the contents

   d) surprise your teacher.

3 If apparatus gets chipped or broken

   a) just keep working

   b) immediately dispose of it

   c) ask the lab assistant for other apparatus

   d) inform the teacher immediately.

4 When using cutting apparatus such as scalpels, you should NEVER cut

   a) on the lab desk

   b) away from your partner

   c) away from you

   d) towards you.

[4]

5 Examine the image below and write SIX activities that should not be done in the lab.

i) _____

ii) _____

iii) _____

iv) _____

v) _____

vi) _____

[6]

2 Scientific measurement and SI units

2.1 Measurement

1 Complete the following table with the correct measurement information.

PHYSICAL QUANTITY	SI UNIT	SYMBOL	ONE INSTRUMENT USED TO MEASURE THIS QUANTITY
length		m	
	kilogram		balance
time		s	
	kelvin		thermometer

[4]

2 Why is it necessary to measure? _____

_____

_____

[2]

3 Choose from the list of these measurements the most appropriate to measure each of the given quantities.

millilitre millimetre litre kilogram gram kilometre centimetre metre

a) The mass of a fridge. _____

b) The length of a pencil. _____

c) The mass of an apple. _____

d) The amount in a drop of water. _____

e) The distance from Trinidad to New York. _____

f) The length of an ant. _____

g) The height of the school building. _____

h) The amount of water in a bucket. _____

[8]

Circle the correct answer in questions 4–5.

4 On your lunch table you have a small glass, a paper napkin, a ceramic plate and a metal fork. List the items in order from the lightest to the heaviest:

a) napkin, fork, plate, glass   b) napkin, plate, fork, glass

c) napkin, fork, glass, plate   d) napkin, glass, fork, plate.

5 A cake costs $2.98. About how much change would you get back if you paid with a $5.00 bill?

a) $1.00   b) $2.00   c) $3.00   d) $0.50

[2]

2.2 Measuring length

1 The SI unit for measuring length is _____

[1]

2 What causes parallax errors in measuring? _____

_____

[2]

3 Give TWO situations where you would need callipers for measuring length.

_____

_____

[2]

4 Over the ruler below, draw external callipers showing the measurement of 5 cm.

[4]

[Box for drawing]

5 In the box above, draw lines of the following lengths using a ruler.

a) 2 cm   **b)** 3.8 cm   **c)** 75 mm

[3]

2.3   Measuring volume of liquids

1 The volume of a liquid is the _____ it occupies.

[1]

2 The volume of a liquid is measured in _____.

[1]

3 One cm^3 = _____ ml.

[1]

4 To find the volume of a liquid a scientist uses a _____.

[1]

5 Is the meniscus shown in this test tube a convex meniscus or a concave meniscus?

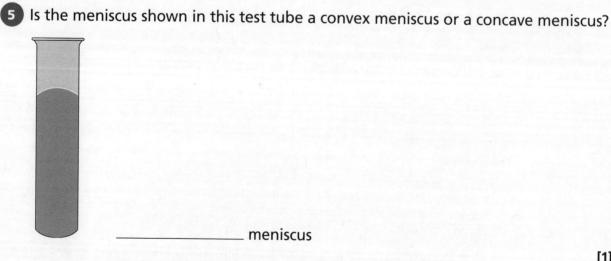

_____ meniscus

[1]

6 To measure the volume of a liquid you must read the top of the _____

meniscus or the bottom of the _____ meniscus.

[2]

7 When water is in a test tube it has a _____ meniscus.

[1]

2.4 Measuring the volume of a solid object

1 The method by which the volume of an irregular solid can be found is _____

_____

_____ .

[1]

2 You have found a small stone. Explain to your friends how you would find its
volume. Remember to include any precautions that must be taken.

_____

_____

_____

_____

_____

[5]

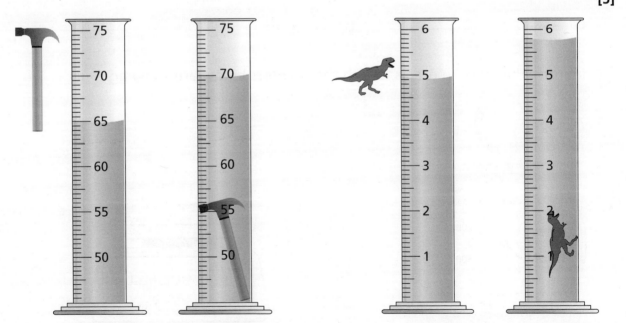

3 The volume of the hammer is _____ cm³.

4 The volume of the toy dinosaur is _____ cm³.

[4]

17

2.5 Measuring mass

1 The SI unit for measuring mass is _____.

[1]

2 What does the mass of an object indicate? _____

_____

[1]

3 Name one thing that is weighed using each of these balances.

a) 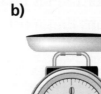   b)   c)    d)

a) _____   b) _____

c) _____   d) _____

[4]

4 Identify the mass, in grams, which the pointers below are showing.

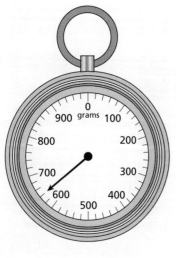

a) _____   b) _____

[2]

2.6 Measuring time

1 The SI unit for time is _____ .

[1]

2 Using linking lines, match the activity being carried out with the type of timepiece needed for recording depending on how accurate the time measurement must be.

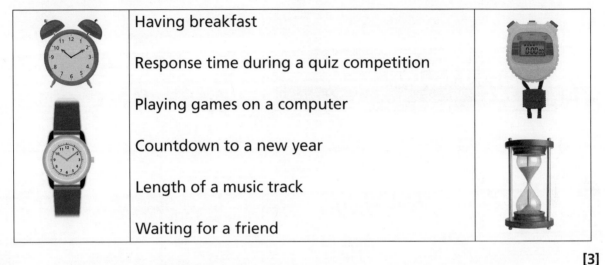

	Having breakfast	
	Response time during a quiz competition	
	Playing games on a computer	
	Countdown to a new year	
	Length of a music track	
	Waiting for a friend	

[3]

3 Read the following scenario on time and complete the quiz that follows.

Alison woke up at 6:15 a.m. After 17 minutes she got to the bathroom and had an 11-minute shower. At 7:04 a.m. she was dressed. She went to breakfast at 7:12 a.m. and immediately after breakfast she left for school at 7:35 a.m.

a) Alison went to the bathroom at _____ .

[1]

b) Alison took _____ minutes to get dressed.

[1]

c) i) How many minutes are there between 7:04 and 7:12? _____

[1]

ii) Suggest TWO activities you think Alison could have done in that time.

_____

_____

[2]

2.7 Measuring temperature

1 Identify the type of thermometer shown.

a) _____ b) _____

[2]

2

On the left side of this thermometer, label the parts indicated by the label lines.

[3]

3 On the right side of the thermometer, show:

a) The boiling point of pure water.

b) The freezing point of ice.

c) The normal body temperature.

[3]

3 Characteristics of living things

3.1 Things can be similar and different

1 Using the word search below, find the seven characteristics that make the difference between living and non-living things.

[7]

```
L  P  T  N  E  M  E  V  O  M  N  Q
F  A  N  J  O  J  M  Y  H  L  X  U
T  Q  K  N  U  T  R  I  T  I  O  N
O  B  E  K  W  Q  V  F  K  L  R  L
M  P  O  M  Q  P  J  W  G  A  Q  B
N  O  I  T  A  R  I  P  S  E  R  Y
U  B  T  H  T  W  O  R  G  Z  I  I
I  R  R  I  T  A  B  I  L  I  T  Y
Q  Y  E  G  Z  G  C  G  A  R  H  B
U  G  F  G  D  G  W  S  O  G  I  D
N  O  I  T  E  R  C  X  E  Q  O  E
N  O  I  T  C  U  D  O  R  P  E  R
```

2 All living things are composed of _____.

[1]

3 While most organisms are multicellular, there are many that are _____

_____.

[1]

4 Use the diagram to show TWO similarities and TWO differences between plants and animals.

[4]

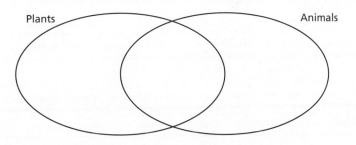

Plants   Animals

3.2 Growth

1 Growth is defined as _____

_____

_____.

[1]

2 As some living things grow, such as frogs, they undergo a process called

_____

_____.

[1]

3 Examine this illustration of the growth of a human from a toddler to maturity and answer the questions that follow.

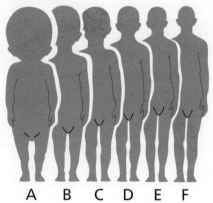

A   B   C   D   E   F

a) Which part of the body grows the most? _____

[1]

b) What fraction of the length of the body of A is the head? _____

[2]

c) What fraction of the length of the body of F is the head? _____

[2]

d) Explain what happens to the proportion of the head to the body as an individual develops from A to F.

_____

_____

_____

_____

[3]

3.3 Respiration

1 The exchange of gases in the lungs is referred to as

_____.

[1]

2 The process by which cells produce energy is described as

_____.

[1]

3 Convert the following information on respiration to a chemical equation.

"In order to obtain energy, glucose and oxygen enter the cell and react, releasing carbon dioxide, which is expelled from the cell."

_____

[2]

4 In unicellular organisms and plants the uptake of oxygen is carried out by the simple process of diffusion. In mammals, the process of delivering oxygen to the cells requires the help of the internal transport system called the

_____.

[1]

5 The rate of respiration varies. Name ONE way in which the rate can increase.

_____

[1]

6 State whether the following statements are TRUE or FALSE.

a) Plants can choose whether they use or expel carbon dioxide.   _____

b) Every organism needs a complex circulatory system.   _____

c) In sunlight, the rate of photosynthesis is greater than
the rate of respiration.   _____

d) The main purpose of respiration is to release energy.   _____

e) Both carbon dioxide and oxygen enter the plant
through its leaves.   _____

[5]

3.4 Irritability

1 Irritability means sensitivity and it is the ability of a living thing to

_____

_____ .

[1]

2 In the table, name TWO environmental influences that a living thing may be sensitive to and give ONE way it may react to each influence.

	ENVIRONMENTAL INFLUENCE	REACTION
1		
2		

[4]

3 The names of the sense organs are given in the table. Identify ONE stimulus received by each sense organ.

SENSE ORGAN	STIMULUS
Eyes	
Ears	
Nose	
Tongue	
Skin	

[5]

4 People may say "As blind as a bat", but bats fly and do not crash into walls. Why is this?

_____

_____

_____

_____

[3]

3.5 Movement

1 Choose whether the following statements are TRUE or FALSE.

a) Movement is the ability to change any position of the body. _____

b) All animals move in the same way. _____

c) Snakes and fish have no legs so they depend highly on the strength of their muscles for movement. _____

d) All birds have wings that assist them with movement. _____

e) Of all known animals, centipedes have the most legs. _____

[5]

2 Plants do not move voluntarily. Name ONE stimulus that makes plants move.

_____

[1]

3.6 Nutrition

1 Nutrition is concerned with _____.

[1]

2 Green plants produce food using the process of _____.

[1]

3 To obtain nutrients some animals eat plants only and are called _____

_____.

[1]

4 Animals that eat flesh only are called _____.

[1]

5 Why is it necessary for carnivores to have sharp front teeth?

_____

_____.

[2]

6 Crows and vultures are scavengers. Their nutrition consists of _____

_____.

[1]

7 The nutrition of omnivores includes both _____

and _____ material.

[2]

3.7 Excretion

1 Excretion is defined as _____

_____.

[1]

2 What is the name given to the process of the removal of undigested waste from the gut?

_____

[1]

3 In unicellular organisms and plants excretion is a simple process. In complex mammals, the process requires the help of the _____

_____ which expels waste from the body.

[1]

4 Decide whether the following statements are TRUE or FALSE.

a) Faeces are the result of excretion. _____

b) Urine is the result of excretion. _____

c) Cell sap is a result of plant excretion. _____

d) All waste leaving the human body is the result of excretion. _____

e) Egested material comes from over-worked body cells. _____

f) Both egesting and excretion are concerned with getting rid of body waste. _____

[6]

3.8 Reproduction

1 Reproduction means _____.

[1]

2 There are two types of reproduction, asexual and _____.

[1]

3 Simple organisms with just one cell reproduce by _____ as there is only one parent.

[1]

4 Binary fission and vegetative reproduction are two examples of _____ reproduction.

[1]

5 During sexual reproduction in plants, the male sex cells, called _____, are transferred to the _____ parts. This process is called _____. The pollen then combines with female _____ cells, eventually producing seeds.

[4]

6 Some animals have both male and female sex organs. These animals are called

_____.

[1]

4.1 Cells

1 Cells are defined as _____.

[1]

2 Cells have different shapes because they perform different _____.

[1]

3 Yeast used for making bread is a _____ fungus.

[1]

4 A microscope must be used to see a cell because _____

_____.

[1]

5 Name the parts of the microscope indicated by the labelling lines in this diagram.

[6]

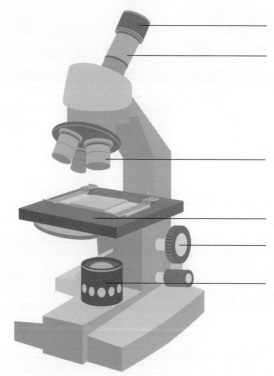

6 Why is dye placed on the cells? _____

_____.

[1]

7 Identify and name the parts of the animal cell below indicated by adding labels to the lines on this diagram.

[5]

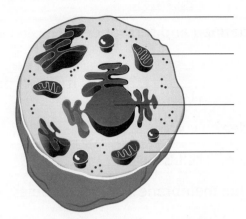

8 All the information of a cell is in the DNA of the chromosomes. In what part of the cell are the chromosomes found? _____

[1]

9 Here is a model of a typical plant cell.

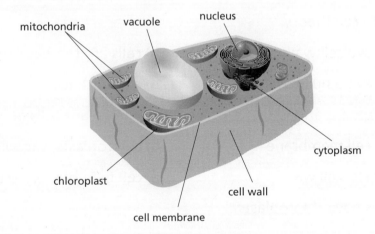

a) Identify TWO differences between a plant and an animal cell.

i) _____

[1]

ii) _____

[1]

10 a) What is responsible for the green colour of a plant? _____

b) What other purpose does the green colouring have? _____

_____

[2]

11 A cell which is well defined and surrounded by a cell wall is a/an _____ cell.

[1]

12 The cell membrane is _____ as it allows passage of only some solutes.

[1]

For questions 13–24, circle the correct answer.

13 The tough boundary of a cell is called

a) the wall   b) the membrane   c) globules   d) the cytoplasm.

14 Which of the following is NOT found in animal cells?

a) Vacuole   b) Mitochondria   c) Chloroplasts   d) Nucleus

15 What is the jellylike region inside a cell called?

a) Vacuole   b) Cytoplasm   c) Nucleus   d) Chloroplast

16 According to cell theory:

a) all cells have cell walls   b) cells are the basic unit of living things

c) all cells have a nucleus   d) all cells have a rigid structure.

17 Both _____ and _____ are found in plant cells only.

a) cell wall, cell membrane   b) chloroplasts, vacuole

c) chloroplasts, cell wall   d) cell membrane, vacuole

18 Why do cells have chloroplasts?

a) To contain chlorophyll.   b) To regulate the functions of the cell.

c) To assist with respiration.   d) To keep the cytoplasm contained.

19 What is the function of the cell membrane?

a) Storing food, water and waste.   b) Controlling cell activity.

c) Holding the cell together.   d) Absorbing light energy.

20 What is the function of the nucleus?

a) Storing food, water and waste.   b) Controlling cell activity.

c) Holding the cell together.   d) Absorbing light energy.

21 What is the function of the vacuole?

    a) Storing food, water and waste.   **b)** Controlling cell activity.

    c) Holding the cell together.   **d)** Absorbing light energy.

22 The mitochondria are

    a) storage spaces for food   **b)** control centres

    c) powerhouses   **d)** glucose manufacturers.

23 What is the function of the cell wall?

    a) To contain chlorophyll.   **b)** To give the cell its rigid structure.

    c) To control what enters the cell.   **d)** To allow only water to enter the cell.

24 Which of the following is NOT a function of the vacuole in a plant cell?

    a) Helping to maintain the structure of the cell.

    b) Containing waste material.

    c) Transferring unwanted materials out of the cell.

    d) Protecting the chloroplasts.

                                                              [12]

25 Say whether each of the following is TRUE or FALSE.

    a) Robert Hooke observed cork cells under a microscope.   _____

    b) You can see most cells without any extra equipment.   _____

    c) All living things are composed of many cells.   _____

    d) Animal cells can also be found in humans.   _____

    e) A small number of living things are made of units which are not cells.   _____

    f) The mitochondria are the cell's main storage area.   _____

    g) The large vacuole is found in plant cells only.   _____

    h) All living organisms are multicellular.   _____

    i) Only animal cells have chloroplasts.   _____

    j) The cell wall protects the animal cell from damage.   _____

    k) Plant leaf cells contain more chlorophyll than other parts.   _____

    l) Solar energy is used to build carbohydrates in the mitochondria.   _____

                                                              [12]

5.1   Cells, tissues and organs

1 Complete this flow chart to show the organization of the body's building blocks.

[4]

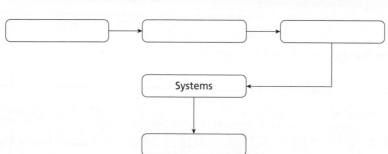

2 Name THREE body systems.

a) _____

b) _____

c) _____

[3]

3 Which organisms are made of organ systems?

_____

[1]

5.2   Respiratory system

1 Add the labels to this diagram to name the parts of the respiratory system.

[5]

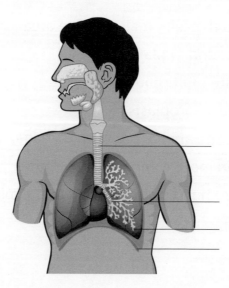

2 In which part of the lungs are oxygen and carbon dioxide exchanged?

_____

[1]

3 When you inhale, the volume of the lungs _____ .

[1]

4 Look at this diagram of a model of the respiratory system.

    a) Label the structures indicated to show what parts of the respiratory system they represent.

[4]

    b) Name TWO parts of the respiratory system not represented in this model.

_____

_____

[2]

5.3   Circulatory system

1 What is the circulatory system responsible for? _____

_____

_____

[1]

2 Why is it necessary for the arteries to be thick and muscular? _____

_____

[2]

3 What information does the pulse rate give? _____

_____

[1]

4 Why does the blood travel back to the heart?

_____

[1]

5 Which organ is at the centre of the circulatory system? _____

[1]

6 The vessels that carry blood back to the heart are called _____ .

[1]

5.4   Digestive system

1 What is the purpose of the digestive system? _____

[1]

2 The first place digestion occurs in the body is the _____ .

[1]

Use this diagram to answer questions 3–6.

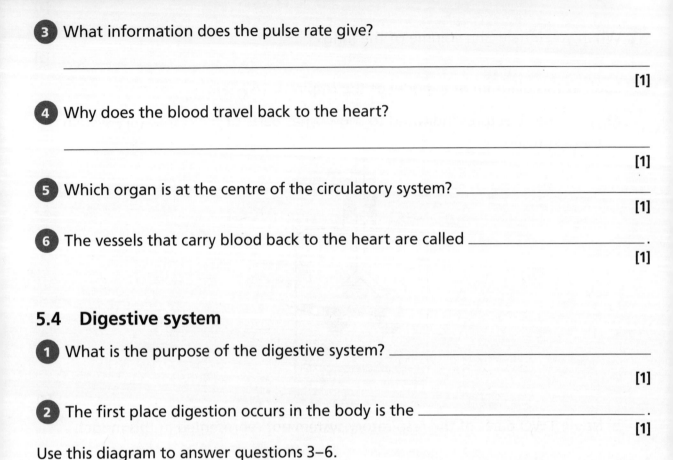

3 Which system is represented by this diagram?

    a) Nervous   **b)** Digestive   **c)** Alimentary canal

4 On the diagram, A represents:

    a) one lung   **b)** a kidney   **c)** the stomach.

5 The function of C is to:

    a) absorb water   **b)** add chemicals to faeces   **c)** keep the gut contained.

6 What happens in D?

    a) Digestion is completed.   **b)** Toxins are neutralized.

    c) Alcohol absorption occurs.

5.5 Excretory system

1 What is excretion? _____

_____
      [1]

2 The removal of undigested waste from the body is called _____.
      [1]

3 Name the parts of the excretory system by adding the missing labels.

      [5]

4 Circle the substances in this list that are the result of excretion.

      SWEAT   VOMIT   CARBON DIOXIDE

         URINE   BLOOD   FAECES

      [3]

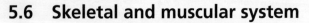
5.6   Skeletal and muscular system

1 The muscular system is responsible for the muscles. The skeletal system is responsible for

_____ .

[1]

2 Name TWO parts of the skeletal system that provide protection for body organs.

a) _____

b) _____

[2]

3 What do the muscles assist the bones with? _____

[1]

4 **a)** On this diagram of a skeleton, name and label FIVE of the bones that you know.

[5]

b) Which is the longest bone in the human skeleton? _____

[1]

c) How many bones are there in each lower limb? _____

[1]

d) What can a ball and socket joint do that a hinge joint cannot? _____

_____ .

[1]

5.7 Reproductive system

1 What is the function of the reproductive system? _____

_____

[1]

2 Some parts of the male and female reproductive systems in these diagrams are identified by letters. Write the letter next to the correct name given in the tables that follow.

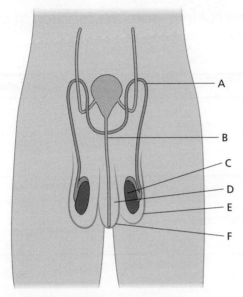
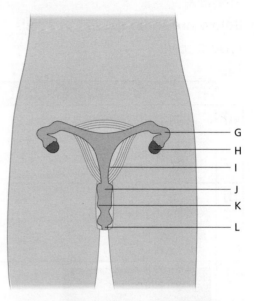

Male reproductive system

PART	LETTER
penis	
sperm duct	
testis	
urethra	
foreskin	
scrotum	

Female reproductive system

PART	LETTER
oviduct	
ovary	
uterine lining	
vagina	
cervix	
opening of vagina	

[6]

3 The male sex organs are the _____ and they

produce _____ while the female sex organs are

_____ and they produce _____.

[4]

5.8 Specialized animal cells

1 What is a specialized cell?

_____ .

[1]

2 Below are some specialized cells. In the second column write the function of each type of cell.

[3]

	SPECIALIZED CELL	FUNCTION
a)		
b)		
c)		
d)		
e)		
f)		

3 Name each specialized cell in the table.

a) _____   b) _____

c) _____   d) _____

e) _____   f) _____

[6]

5.9 Plant systems

1 Look at this diagram of a plant. Label the four parts, A, B, C and D.

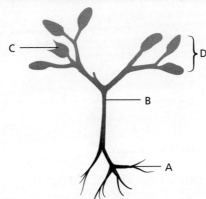

[4]

2 Give ONE purpose for each part of a flowering plant.

Stem: _____

Root: _____

Leaves: _____

Flowers: _____

[4]

3 What process cannot happen if a plant has no chlorophyll? _____

[1]

5.10 Specialized plant cells

1 Why do the palisade cells of the plant have dense chloroplasts? _____

_____

[1]

2 The guard cells are on the underside of the leaf of a plant. Why are they called

guard cells? _____

_____

[1]

3 What is the advantage of having root hairs? _____

_____

[1]

6 Cellular processes – diffusion

6.1 Diffusion

1 Diffusion is _____

_____.

[1]

For questions 2–7, circle the correct answer.

2 Which of the following does not affect diffusion?

  a) Breeze   **b)** Gravity   **c)** Movement   **d)** Evaporation

[1]

3 As the temperature increases, the rate of diffusion:

  a) increases   **b)** decreases

  c) remains the same   **d)** dries out the cell.

[1]

4 Which substance diffuses into respiring cells?

  a) Oxygen   **b)** Carbon dioxide   **c)** Starch   **d)** Chlorophyll

[1]

5 In which state/s of matter can diffusion occur?

  a) Liquid   **b)** Liquid and gas   **c)** Gas   **d)** Solid

[1]

6 Which substance other than oxygen diffuses into the cells?

  a) Carbon dioxide   **b)** Glucose

  c) Nitrogen   **d)** Chlorophyll

[1]

7 When the concentration of a substance inside the cell is greater than the concentration outside the cell, a substance moves:

  a) out of the cell   **b)** into the cell

  c) stays suspended inside the cell   **d)** into the nucleus.

[1]

6.2 Osmosis

1 Osmosis is defined as _____

_____

_____.

[1]

For questions 2–4, circle the correct answer.

2 The cell wall is:

a) partially permeable   b) fully permeable

c) non-permeable   d) waterproof.

[1]

3 Which term describes the cell membrane?

a) Non-permeable   b) Partially permeable

c) Fully permeable   d) Rigid

[1]

4 The diagram below shows solutions of different concentrations in A and B.

A	B
3·0 g/cm³	1·5 g/cm³

In which direction will the solution flow?

a) A to B.

b) B to A.

c) A is bigger than B – no flow will occur.

d) There will be no movement.

[1]

6.3 Photosynthesis

1 Photosynthesis is _____

_____.

[1]

2 For photosynthesis, plants take in carbon dioxide through their

_____ and water through their _____.

[2]

3 The products of photosynthesis are _____ and _____.

[2]

4 Photosynthesis and respiration are the _____ of each other since photosynthesis is a building-up process and respiration is a breakdown process.

[1]

5 The products of respiration are _____ and

_____.

[2]

Circle the correct answer in questions 6–8.

6 Which of the following is needed for photosynthesis?

a) Glucose   **b)** Water   **c)** Oxygen   **d)** Starch

[1]

7 Which of the following does NOT affect photosynthesis?

a) Heat   **b)** Light   **c)** Water   **d)** Pressure

[1]

8 When do plants respire?

a) All the time.   **b)** At night time.

c) Mostly on rainy days.   **d)** After photosynthesis.

[1]

9 The food made during photosynthesis is stored as _____ in the plant.

[1]

10 Explain why photosynthesis is important to humans. _____

_____

[2]

7.1 Matter

1 Classify the pictures on the left under one of the headings on the right based on their state of matter.

[6]

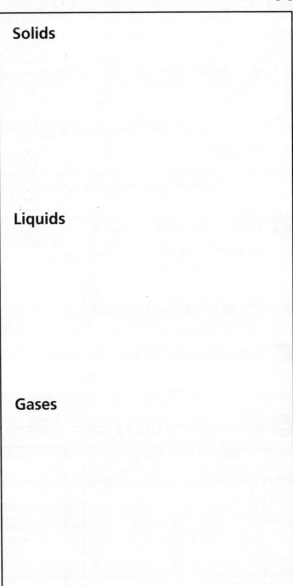

Solids

Liquids

Gases

2 States of matter are physical properties because _____

_____.

[2]

7.2 – 7.4 States of matter

1 Give two properties of each state of matter.

a) Solids _____

_____

[2]

b) Liquids _____

_____

[2]

c) Gases _____

_____

[2]

2 What common property do:

a) solids and liquids have? _____

[1]

b) liquids and gases have? _____

[1]

3 Both the volume and the shape of matter depend on the _____

_____ between their particles.

[1]

4 In each of the spaces below draw particles to represent each state of matter.

a) Solid   **b)** Liquid   **c)** Gas

[3]

7.5 Particle theory

1 All matter is made up of _____

_____.

[2]

2 As the amount of energy in matter increases, the bonds between its particles

_____

_____.

[1]

3 For each pair below, circle the state in which the particles have greater energy.

a)   b)   c)

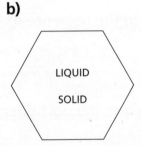
LIQUID

GAS

LIQUID

SOLID

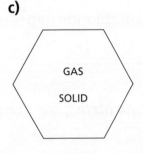
GAS

SOLID

[3]

4 State whether each of the following is TRUE or FALSE.

a) When a solid melts its particles slowly cease to exist. _____

b) A solid can stay in one place because its particles are at rest.

_____

c) When you increase the temperature, the speed of particles will increase.

_____

[3]

5 In which states of matter:

a) are particles randomly arranged? _____

b) can squeezing or compressing occur? _____

c) is there the least attraction between particles? _____

d) are there neatly arranged particles held by strong bonds? _____

[4]

7.6 – 7.8   Melting and solidifying

1 Melting is the change from _____ to _____.

[2]

2 The temperature of ice is below _____ °C.

[1]

3 As ice melts, its temperature _____.

[1]

4 Dry cobalt chloride paper is blue. In the presence of water it changes to

_____.

[1]

5 As melting occurs, the bonds between the particles of a solid _____.

[1]

6 Solidifying is the change of state from _____ to

_____.

[2]

7 As a liquid solidifies, the bonds between its particles _____.

[1]

8 On each arrow, indicate whether heat is gained or lost as a substance melts or solidifies.

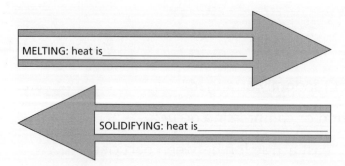

MELTING: heat is_____

SOLIDIFYING: heat is_____

[2]

9 When matter melts or solidifies, do its chemical properties change? _____

[1]

7.9 Evaporation and condensation

1 When a liquid evaporates, it changes to a _____.

[1]

2 Evaporation occurs as the temperature _____.

[1]

3 The bonds between the particles _____ when a liquid becomes a gas.

[1]

4 When matter condenses, its state changes from _____ to

_____.

[2]

5 As condensation occurs, the change in energy of the particles causes them to

come closer and form _____.

[1]

6 To show that water does not change after condensation, we use _____

_____ paper, which turns from blue to pink.

[1]

7 For each arrow below, indicate whether heat is gained or lost as evaporation or condensation occurs.

a) Evaporation:

heat is _____.

b) Condensation:

heat is _____.

[2]

8 Evaporation and condensation are _____ changes since the substance of matter does not change.

[1]

9 Examine this diagram of the water cycle.

a) Which number represents evaporation? _____

[1]

b) Number _____ represents condensation.

[1]

c) Describe the process occurring at 4.

_____

_____

_____

_____

7.10 Sublimation

1 When matter sublimes it changes from _____ to _____.

[2]

2 Since no new substance is formed, sublimation is a _____ process.

[1]

3 Solid _____ _____ is known as dry ice.

[1]

4 Because dry ice sublimes, give one advantage of using it on a stage during a concert. _____

_____

[1]

5 Desublimation occurs when a substance changes from a _____ to

a _____ .

[2]

6 Decide whether the following statements are TRUE or FALSE.

a) Sublimation is an example of a change of state. _____

b) As substances sublimate, their particles have less energy. _____

c) Whenever water ice gains heat, it undergoes sublimation. _____

d) When solid air fresheners shrink, it is because they undergo sublimation.

_____

[4]

7 On each arrow indicate whether heat is gained or lost as sublimation or desublimation occurs.

[2]

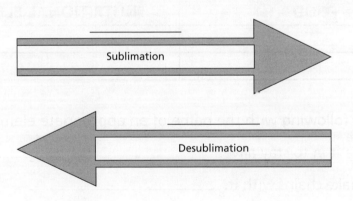

Sublimation

Desublimation

8.1 Matter's building blocks

1 Matter's building blocks are called elements. How is an element defined?

_____

[1]

2 The elements are arranged in a chart called _____.

[1]

3 Every element has a _____ consisting of 1, 2 or 3 letters.

[1]

4 Of the 118 elements name:

a) Two metals: _____

[2]

b) Two gases: _____

[2]

c) Two non-metals: _____

[2]

5 Identify TWO foods and give ONE nutritional element each carries.

FOOD	NUTRITIONAL ELEMENT

[4]

6 Complete the following with the name of an appropriate element.

a) You breathe it in to stay alive. _____

b) Jewellers make chains with it. _____

c) It is placed in thermometers. _____

d) It is used on cuts and bruises. _____

e) It is used for making coloured lights. _____

[5]

7 Can you find the first 20 elements in this periodic table?

Find an element

```
F E                                          N X
Y N                                          D X
T I A G                            D E A F B N R R E P Q I
Z F J L                            A G H P T I E P I Z O R
C D N S                            F J O K A T E G I A S O
T H D L                            J J T R Z R F P Y M S A
X K I L K Y U N L I T H I U M S X M A G N E S I U M G F D O N R D X A K
A L U M I N I U M M Y E Y R C H G S N V K Z K O S O L M Q G U O H F O L
O F Z O X B K L Z K S M U I S S A T O P C A H A N U W E H E G Q R K F K
Q S Q F T N O C I L I S V V M U I C L A C W G L O M Y Z B N X Y V O N V
C H L O R I N E W K X S O D I U M M U I L L Y R E B X J Q G S K J S B P
W R C A R B O N T B G I D I S M P J C N D V I S P N E G O R D Y H I G S
N C G R G Q Q D Z E Y Z Y R D I M A A C R N B B S Q F G U A O M N X P B
A H S V Y G S U R O H P S O H P N O E N E E M U Z F Y K Z N R C N H I X
```

```
V B Z E X S Z X J N C L S K O A O A W N M K I F M U O X X Z
U P V P B O R C Q M Z H Z L E I M U I L E H J O Q M X H T D
```

```
Z Z Z D W F G N W S A C E Y A R U F L U S N C E P P O V F I
H C T N Z C C N E D Q A B G E Y X M G O Y O J K N G A D L B
```

[10]

8.2 Atoms

1 An atom is _____

_____.

[1]

2 Inside every atom are tiny particles called _____ particles.

[1]

3 Draw a model of an atom using this information:

a) Nucleus with protons (p) and neutrons (n).

b) Two shells, each with two electrons (e).

[5]

4 Choose which answer matches the particle with its charge. Put A, B or C in the boxes in the table on the right.

	PARTICLE
A	neutron (n)
B	proton (p)
C	electron (e)

	CHARGE
	−1
	0
	+1

[3]

5 Use the following information to complete the table on subatomic particles.

For every atom, Z = #p = #e and #p + #n = M

Z	#p	#e	#n	M
7			7	
	15		16	
		1		1
	18			40

[6]

8.3 Looking more closely at the periodic table

Here is a diagram of the periodic table for the first 20 elements.

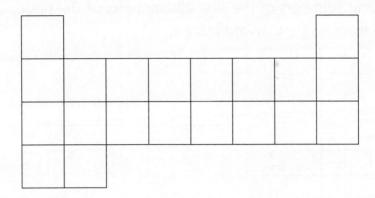

1 Examine the periodic table and answer these questions.

a) There are _____ rows and _____ columns.

[2]

b) The rows are called _____.

[1]

c) The columns are called _____.

[1]

2 Write the group numbers at the top of the periodic table diagram.

[2]

3 Write the period numbers on the left of the periodic table diagram.

[2]

4 a) Place the symbol and give the position of the following elements in the periodic table:

boron   sulfur   helium   potassium

b) Insert the symbols of the elements in the following positions:

G8, P2   G1, P2   P3, G4   G1, P1

[4]

5 All the elements in the same group have similar _____.

[1]

6 Given the atomic numbers of the first 20 elements of the periodic table below, complete the following crossword puzzle.

Across
1. Eleven
4. Seventeen
5. Four
7. Twelve
9. Fifteen
13. Eighteen
17. Twenty
18. Seven
19. Ten
20. Six

Down
2. Eight
3. Thirteen
6. Nine
8. Nineteen
10. One
11. Fourteen
12. Three
14. Sixteen
15. Five
16. Two

[10]

8.4 Electron shells

1 The _____ number indicates the number of shells there are in an atom.

[1]

2 From the first 20 elements, how many atoms have:

a) 1 shell only? _____

b) 2 shells only? _____

c) 3 shells only? _____

d) 4 shells only? _____

[4]

3 An atom has 2 shells only. How many possible groups can it be placed into?

_____

[1]

4 As the number of shells increases, what do you notice about the distance between the nucleus and the outermost shell?

_____

_____

[1]

8.5 Electronic configuration (1)

1 Electronic configuration is concerned with _____

_____.

[2]

2 What is the maximum number of electrons that can be on the:

a) first shell? _____   b) second shell? _____

c) third shell? _____   d) fourth shell? _____

[4]

3 On this periodic table, complete the electronic configuration of these atoms.

a) Beryllium   b) Sulfur   c) Aluminium

d) Argon   e) Hydrogen   f) Nitrogen

H							He
Li	Be	B	C	N	O	F	Ne
Na	Mg	Al	Si	P	S	Cl	Ar

[6]

8.6   Electronic configuration (2)

1 The number of elements on the outermost shell of an atom is the same as _____

_____.

[1]

2 Write the numerical configuration for these atoms.

a) _____   b) _____   c) _____   [3]

3 An element has electronic configuration 2.8.7.

a) Its atomic number is _____.

b) It is in period _____.

c) It belongs in group _____.

d) It has _____ shells.

e) It has _____ electrons in its outermost shell.

f) Its name is _____.

g) Its symbol is _____.

[7]

9 Compounds and mixtures

9.1 Elements, mixtures and compounds

1 When elements combine chemically, each one is not easily identifiable because they form a _____.

[1]

2 Two elements that do not combine are easily separated because they form a

_____.

[1]

3 When a mixture is _____, it may change to form a compound.

[1]

4 Two elements are combined and heated. Suddenly a green flame appears. This may indicate that a _____ reaction has occurred.

[1]

In each of questions 5–9, circle the correct response.

5 How many different atoms are there in a compound?

   a) Always two   **b)** One   **c)** At least two

6 Water is:

   a) an element   **b)** a mixture   **c)** a compound.

7 The air we breathe is:

   a) an element   **b)** a mixture   **c)** a compound.

8 An element is a simple pure substance which:

   a) cannot form a molecule

   b) cannot be split up further

   c) can split apart.

9 Are the properties of a compound identical to those of the elements that make it up?

   a) Always   **b)** It depends   **c)** Never

[5]

10 Two elements are combined during a chemical reaction. Give THREE changes that could have occurred because of the chemical reaction.

_____

_____

_____

_____

_____

_____

[3]

9.2 Atoms and molecules

1 A molecule is _____

_____.

[1]

2 The written notation representing the number of atoms in a molecule is called

_____.

[1]

3 How many different types of atoms are there in these molecules?

a) MgO _____

b) K_2CO_3 _____

[2]

4 How many atoms are there in these molecules?

a) FeS _____

b) H_2O _____

c) CO_2 _____

d) $CuSO_4$ _____

[4]

5 The diagram below represents a chemical _____ .

Fe + S $\longrightarrow$ FeS

[1]

6 Say whether each statement is TRUE or FALSE.

a) A molecule can be made of different types of atom. _____

b) Some molecules are not made up of atoms. _____

c) Molecules bond chemically to form atoms. _____

d) Molecules are made of specific numbers of atoms. _____

e) Atoms can bond with each other only if they are attracted to each other. _____

f) In a compound, no bonds are formed between atoms. _____

g) Strong bonds are formed when mixtures are made. _____

h) When two identical atoms bond, the substance made is an element. _____

[8]

9.3 Molecules that are elements

1 When two identical atoms bond to form a gas, the gas is _____ .

[1]

2 When many atoms of the same type bond to form a substance, the substance is

said to be _____ .

[1]

3 Write the formula for the following diatomic gases.

a) Chlorine: _____

b) Hydrogen: _____

c) Nitrogen: _____

[3]

4 Decide whether each statement is TRUE or FALSE.

a) A diatomic molecule is an element. _____

b) A polyatomic substance is a compound. _____

c) Oxygen gas is an example of an element. _____

d) Diamond, the hardest substance, is made of only carbon. _____

e) Air is polyatomic since it contains many gases. _____

[5]

10 Forces and energy

10.1 Introduction

1 A force is described as _____

_____.

[1]

2 Mass is the amount of matter in an object but weight is _____

_____.

[1]

3 The pressure exerted by an object on a small area is _____
than the pressure exerted by the same object on a larger area.

[1]

4 Energy is used when a force acts over a _____

_____.

[1]

5 Energy occurs in various forms. Give THREE forms of energy.

a) _____

b) _____

c) _____

[3]

6 Sources of energy that are continually available are referred to as

_____.

[1]

7 Circle the statement below that is correct.

A force cannot cause:

a) an object to speed up or slow down

b) the sea to be calm

c) a cat to see in the dark

d) a lizard to slide down a leaf.

[1]

10.2 Action of forces

1 Give FOUR possible effects on an object when forces act on it.

a) _____

b) _____

c) _____

d) _____

[4]

2 A force can make a stationary object _____.

[1]

3 A car travels _____ when the accelerator is pressed and

_____ when the brake is pressed.

[2]

4 When two cars crash, the body panels of the cars change _____.

[1]

5 For these activities, give your answers on the lines provided.

a) A motor boat speeding on the sea.

What is the force? _____

What is the body applying the force? _____

What is the body receiving the force? _____

What is the effect of the force? _____

[4]

b) The weight of a baby on the cradle mattress.

What is the force? _____

What is the body applying the force? _____

What is the body receiving the force? _____

What is the effect of the force? _____

[4]

10.3 Types of forces

1 State whether these actions are caused by PUSH or PULL forces.

a) Putting on your socks. _____

b) Throwing some water. _____

c) Opening an umbrella. _____

d) Zipping up your coat. _____

[4]

In questions 2–7, choose the correct answer.

2 The force that acts on bodies in physical contact with each other is:

a) gravitational　　b) friction　　c) magnetic　　d) electrostatic.

[1]

3 The force attracting a body to Earth is:

a) magnetic　　b) electrostatic　　c) frictional　　d) gravitational.

[1]

4 The force which exists between charged particles is:

a) frictional　　b) electrostatic　　c) magnetic　　d) gravitational.

[1]

5 The force between the Earth's poles is:

a) magnetic　　b) electrostatic　　c) frictional　　d) gravitational.

[1]

6 Buoyancy is an example of a _____ force.

a) non-contact　　b) contact　　c) magnetic　　d) gravitational

[1]

7 Air resistance is a _____ force.

a) non-contact　　b) magnetic　　c) contact　　d) electrostatic

[1]

10 Forces and energy (cont.)

10.4 Friction

1 How do frictional forces occur? _____

_____

[1]

2 Indicate whether these statements are TRUE or FALSE.

a) When an object slides there is less friction than when it rolls.

_____

b) Butter requires a great deal of friction to slide on a hot cookie tray.

_____

c) Car tyres have grips to help them stop._____

d) Grease and wax are used to increase friction._____

[4]

3 Why is there so much friction in sandpaper? Choose the correct answer.

a) Its surface will get smooth.

b) It can cause rough surfaces to get smooth.

c) It should not be used on tiles.

d) Its surface is very rough.

[1]

4 Why are oil and grease used by people who mend bikes? Choose the correct answer.

a) To get a faster ride.

b) To reduce friction between the tyres and the road.

c) To get the parts moving smoothly.

d) To encourage the cyclists to ride slower.

[1]

5 Circle the activities below that involve the use of frictional force.

writing

smelling a fruit

the Earth in orbit

falling off a tree

a plane taking off

stopping a ball

scrubbing a pot

a dripping tap

a tyre skidding

dragging a toy

water surfing

blowing up a balloon

[6]

10.5   Water resistance and air resistance

1 Ships are heavy but they remain afloat because of _____.

[1]

Circle the correct answer for questions 2–3.

2 Why do parachutists not fall to the ground quickly?

a) They are too light for the air.

b) They know how to ride the air waves.

c) There is air resistance.

d) The air is very dense with water droplets.

[1]

3 The effect that water resistance has on a swimmer is that:

a) he is slowed down

b) he swims with the tide

c) he swims with the water currents

d) he uses an oxygen tank for breathing.

[1]

4 Water resistance is a _____ force.

a) pushing   **b)** pulling   **c)** twisting   **d)** gravitational

[1]

5 In each circle, draw an arrow to show the direction in which air resistance and buoyancy act.

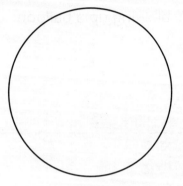

a) Air resistance

b) Buoyancy

[2]

6 Examine the diagram of the two rising hot air balloons. They are exactly the same except for their size.

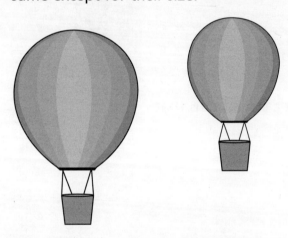

Balloon A   Balloon B

a) Which balloon should rise higher? _____

[1]

b) Using the effect of forces, explain the reason for your response in part **a)**.

_____

_____

_____

[2]

10.6   Representing forces

1 Forces have both size (magnitude) and direction and can be represented by arrows. Compare each pair and say whether the sizes and directions are equal or different by writing YES or NO in the table.

	FORCES	MAGNITUDE	DIRECTION
a)			
b)			
c)			
d)			
e)			
f)			

[6]

Indicate whether the magnitude (M) and direction (D) are EQUAL or DIFFERENT in the following scenarios.

2 Jack walked 5 km north and Jill ran 10 km south.

M _____   D _____

3 Ali and Bjorn competed in a 100 m race. Ali crossed the finish line and Bjorn fainted after 98 m.

M _____   D _____

4 Two teams tied in a tug-of-war competition.

M _____   D _____

[3]

10.7   Resultant of forces acting along the same line

1 The resultant of two forces is found by _____

_____.

[1]

2 One force is seen as positive and the other as negative if _____

_____.

[1]

For questions 3–6, write the missing force over the respective arrows below.

3 $\xrightarrow{\text{8N}}$ + $\xrightarrow{\text{6N}}$ = $\xrightarrow{}$

4 $\xrightarrow{\text{12N}}$ + $\xleftarrow{\text{9N}}$ = $\xrightarrow{}$

5 $\xrightarrow{\text{7N}}$ + $\xrightarrow{}$ = $\xrightarrow{\text{15N}}$

6 $\xrightarrow{}$ + $\xleftarrow{\text{4N}}$ = $\xrightarrow{\text{9N}}$

[4]

Circle the correct answer for questions 7–8.

7 A balanced object does not fall because it is:

    a) affected by equal and opposite forces   **b)** unequal to the force of gravity

    c) not affected by forces   **d)** on a scale.

[1]

8 An example of balanced force is:

    a) speeding up on a slippery road

    b) birds flying in opposite directions

    c) a cyclist displaying stunts

    d) a cup on a chair.

[1]

10.8 Mass and weight

Circle the correct answer for questions 1–4.

1 The mass of a body depends on its:

   a) size   **b)** volume

   c) force   **d)** amount of matter.

2 A body's weight depends on:

   a) the pull of gravity   **b)** its density

   c) its buoyancy   **d)** its volume.

3 All objects of the same weight have:

   a) the same place on Earth

   b) the same mass

   c) the same volume

   d) pull of gravity on them.

4 Inertia is best described as the tendency to:

   a) attract objects   **b)** float

   c) sink   **d)** resist a change of motion.

[4]

Write weight W or mass M for questions 5–9 to indicate what each statement refers to.

5 Measuring the amount of stuff in matter. _____

6 Changing your location on Earth. _____

7 As inertia increases, _____ increases.

8 Using a spring balance. _____

9 Indicates the amount of force. _____

[5]

10.9   Gravity

Circle the correct answer for questions 1–5.

1 Both gravity and friction are examples of:

    a) motion   **b)** forces   **c)** distances   **d)** inertia.

2 A ball tossed into the air falls to the ground because of:

    a) friction   **b)** inertia   **c)** air resistance   **d)** gravity.

3 Gravity acts between any two bodies that have:

    a) weightlessness   **b)** heaviness   **c)** mass   **d)** inertia.

4 When gravity changes _____ changes.

    a) mass   **b)** weight   **c)** force   **d)** friction

5 Which of the diagrams below show gravitational forces?

A   **B**   **C**

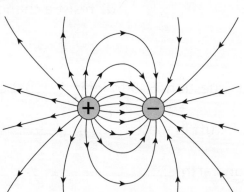
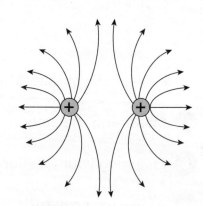

    a) A only   **b)** A and B only

    c) A and C only   **d)** A, B and C

                                                          [5]

10.10   Weight in other places

1 Weight gives the measurement of the force of _____ on an object.

   a) friction   **b)** gravity   **c)** inertia   **d)** attraction

   [1]

This table compares the weight of a given substance on four different planets.
Use the information to answer questions 2–8.

PLANET	ACCELERATION DUE TO GRAVITY IN m/s^2
Mercury	3·6
Earth	9·8
Jupiter	26·0
Neptune	14·1

2 On which planet would the object weigh the most? _____
   _____

3 If a substance has a mass of 100 g on Mercury, what would its mass be on Jupiter?
   _____

4 Earthan lives on Earth. To which planet should he go if he wants his school bag
   to feel lighter?
   _____

5 Junior from Jupiter arrived on Earth this morning. Comparatively, would he be
   stronger or weaker than Earthan? _____
   _____

6 Which 20-year-old boy would you expect to be the tallest, one from Jupiter or
   one from Earth? _____
   _____

7 On which planet is a falling object most likely to break?_____
   _____

8 A substance is taken from Earth to Neptune. How would its measurable
   properties change?

   a) Same density, greater mass.   **b)** Same volume, less weight.

   c) Less weight, greater density.   **d)** Greater weight, same mass.   [7]

10.11   Force and pressure

1 Pressure depends on the amount of _____ on which a force is exerted.

[1]

2 All the shoes shown here belong to the same person. Each shoe has been numbered. The questions are about the shoes when they are being worn. Choose the correct shoe in each case.

1

2

3

4

5

6

Which shoe:

a) exerts the greatest force? _____

b) exerts the least pressure? _____

c) is best for running? _____

d) is most inappropriate for walking on sand? _____

e) is best for ballroom dancing? _____

f) is the most appropriate for walking on sand? _____

[6]

3 The same person applies the same amount of force on the top of the two objects shown. The thumb tack penetrates a board but the walking stick does not. Why is this so?

_____

_____

                                                                              [1]

4 Freshly fallen snow is soft. Explain why the skier shown in the diagram does not go through this type of snow.

_____

_____

                                                                              [1]

5 The relationship between pressure, force and area is given in the formula

$$pressure = \frac{force}{area}$$

Use the formula to find these values.

a) The force exerted on an area of 2.5 m² is 2000 N. Find the pressure. [2]	b) The pressure exerted on an area of 3 m² is 6000 N/m². Find the force exerted. [2]

10.12   Pressure and gases

1 A gas is poured into a container and sealed but there is continuous pressure being created inside.

a) What activity in the sealed container is responsible for that pressure?

_____

_____

[1]

b) If more gas particles were added to the container, what would happen to the pressure?

_____

_____

[1]

c) What would happen if a tiny hole were made in the cover?

_____

_____

_____

[1]

d) If the particles were transferred to a smaller container, explain whether or not there would be a change in the pressure.

_____

_____

_____

_____

[2]

2 Each of these four manometers is attached to a gas chamber as shown by A. The other end of each manometer is open. Examine the manometers and answer the questions that follow.

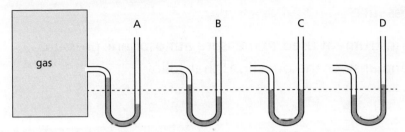

a) What is the pressure of the gas in the chamber being compared with?

_____

[1]

b) The lowest pressure from the gas in the chamber occurs in manometer

_____.

[1]

c) The greatest gas pressure in the chamber occurs in manometer

_____.

[1]

d) Explain why the liquid in the U-tube is level in manometer C. _____

_____

_____

_____

[2]

e) If all the liquid in manometer A entered the gas chamber, what explanation would you provide?

_____

_____

_____

_____

_____

[2]

10.13 Atmospheric pressure

1 This is a diagram of an instrument used to measure atmospheric pressure.
Examine the diagram and answer the questions that follow.

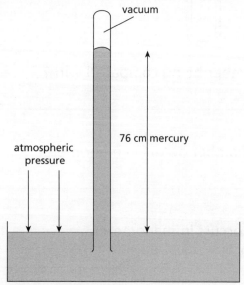

vacuum

76 cm mercury

atmospheric
pressure

a) The name of the instrument is _____.

[1]

b) Normal atmospheric pressure is 760 mm of mercury. What does this mean?

_____

[1]

c) If atmospheric pressure increases, what would happen to the level of the
mercury in the tube?

_____

[1]

d) If the vacuum chamber increases, what would it indicate about the
atmospheric pressure?

_____

[1]

2 Why do you not get crushed under this pressure from the atmosphere? _____

_____

[1]

3 Think of the advantages of atmospheric pressure and describe one thing that

would happen if there were no atmospheric pressure. _____

_____

[1]

10.14   Pressure and liquids

1 The diagram shows jets of water from a
container. Why is the water from the bottom
hole squirting out the furthest?

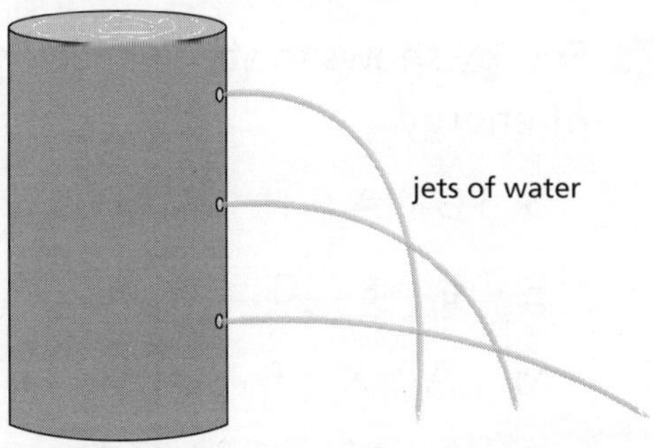

_____

_____

_____

jets of water

[1]

2 The pressure at sea level is 1 atmosphere. As you dive deeper in the sea,

the pressure _____.

[1]

3 A depth of 4 cm of water is poured
into each of these vessels.

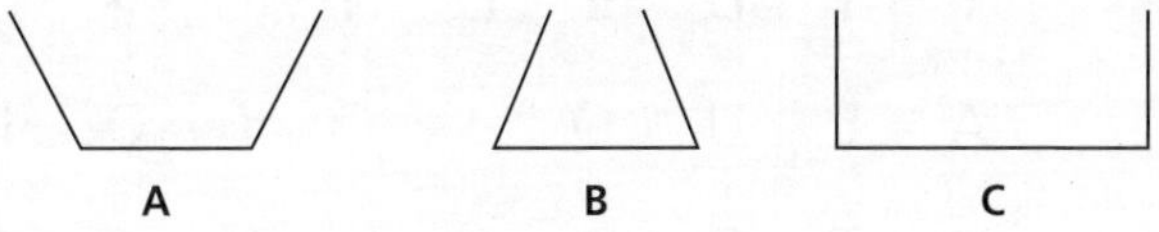

In which vessel will there be:

A   B   C

a) the greatest force acting on its bottom? _____

b) the greatest pressure exerted on its bottom? _____

[2]

4 This diagram shows a model of a dam.

water ——   —— dam

Explain why the base is thicker at the bottom than at the top. _____

_____

[1]

11.1 What is energy?

1 Define 'energy'.

_____

[1]

2 Energy shows in various forms. Use the word search below to find 10 forms of energy.

S	G	A	H	T	H	G	I	L	D	Q	T
E	L	E	C	T	R	I	C	A	L	P	Q
M	A	X	P	O	T	E	N	T	I	A	L
T	E	N	W	L	Z	I	P	D	K	C	M
S	R	C	D	O	V	K	L	N	I	H	A
G	K	A	H	D	O	I	U	I	N	E	G
P	Q	F	E	A	N	K	H	T	E	M	N
Y	T	D	E	L	N	U	K	S	T	I	E
A	L	U	Q	J	C	I	O	H	I	C	T
Y	T	Q	D	L	P	U	C	S	C	A	I
S	U	X	Z	N	O	H	N	A	X	L	C
L	G	F	J	D	B	X	B	E	L	K	H

[5]

3 The term used for stored energy is _____ .

[1]

4 Moving energy is referred to as _____ .

[1]

5 Complete this table by identifying TWO forms of energy that fit under each heading.

SEE	FEEL

[4]

11.2 Potential energy

For each diagram, choose whether it shows the gravitational, chemical or elastic form of potential energy.

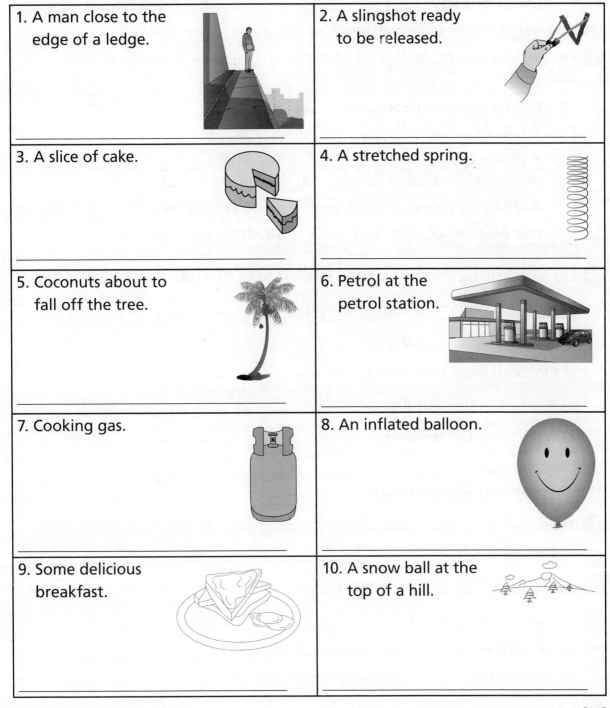

1. A man close to the edge of a ledge.	2. A slingshot ready to be released.
3. A slice of cake.	4. A stretched spring.
5. Coconuts about to fall off the tree.	6. Petrol at the petrol station.
7. Cooking gas.	8. An inflated balloon.
9. Some delicious breakfast.	10. A snow ball at the top of a hill.

[10]

11.3 Kinetic energy

The amount of kinetic energy depends on an object's mass and speed.

1 For each statement, circle the one which has the greater kinetic energy from each pair.

a)	Rolling at the same speed.	b)	Falling from the same height.
	A marble		A chair
	A basket ball		A boulder
c)	Pitching two identical balls.	d)	Travelling in a car.
	Ball 1 by a test match cricketer		At 30 km per hour
	Ball 2 by a 6-year-old child		At 60 km per hour

[4]

2 For each activity, choose whether it refers to POTENTIAL or KINETIC energy.

a) A dove sitting on its eggs in a rooftop nest. _____

b) A lizard climbing up a tree. _____

c) Clothes hanging out on a breezy day. _____

d) A corpse at the morgue. _____

e) A disconnected telephone. _____

[5]

11.4 Heat and light energy

1 The _____ is a source of energy producing both heat and light energy for use on Earth.

[1]

For questions 2–5, circle the correct answer.

2 During the day it is _____ and _____ .

a) hot and fair   b) warm and bright

c) cold and fair   d) bright and cold

[1]

3 When the switch is turned on, a light bulb produces light because

a) its filament gets very hot   b) electricity collects in it

c) it is made of thin glass   d) it needs an outlet for its energy.

[1]

4 If a substance has high kinetic energy it is

a) an electrical conductor

b) a heat conductor

c) burning

d) dazzling.

[1]

5 Which of these statements does *not* describe light?

a) A form of energy which is responsible for the eyes.

b) A form of energy which travels in waves.

c) A form of energy which can cause fire.

d) A form of energy which can travel through water.

[1]

6 Use the word search below to find the 12 words associated with heat and light energy.

```
E   Y   M   R   A   W   E   E
N   D   N   E   B   L   H   L
E   W   A   V   E   S   E   E
R   D   X   V   K   X   A   U
G   B   A   H   S   R   T   F
Y   R   C   O   O   L   A   Y
T   V   L   I   G   H   T   D
T   B   U   R   N   N   U   S
```

[6]

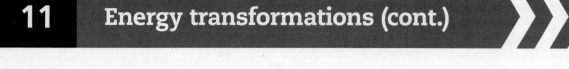

11.5   Sound energy

For questions 1–5, circle the correct answer.

1 Why is there no sound in space?

    a) It is too far for sound to travel.   **b)** Sound waves are absorbed.

    c) There is no matter to carry sound.   **d)** Sound vibrations are too small.

2 Sound waves travel through the air by:

    a) vibrating or moving the particles of matter in the air.

    b) magnetic force.

    c) the force of gravity pulling them to the Earth.

    d) air resistance.

3 When a trumpet is blown, why is a sound heard?

    a) Heat is produced by the trumpeter.

    b) The trumpet reflects sound.

    c) The trumpet causes air to vibrate.

    d) Sound waves are attracted to the trumpet.

4 What does sound travel the fastest through?

    a) Solid   **b)** Liquid   **c)** Gel   **d)** Gas

5 What are sound waves that are regular and organized, making them pleasing to the ear, called?

    a) Music   **b)** Drum beats   **c)** Cacophony   **d)** Noise

[5]

6 Fill in the blanks with the correct word to complete this paragraph.

Sound occurs when objects _____. Vibrating objects pass sounds

to our _____ so we can hear. Sound is able to _____

through matter. In a _____ there is no matter to transmit sound.

The more _____ there are in the vibrations, the louder the sound is.

[5]

11.6   Electrical energy

1 Read the paragraph and use the information to draw a model of a power station. Label each part and identify the activity occurring.

Generating electricity

In many power stations, coal, oil and natural gas are burnt as fuel for generating electricity. A power station consists of three main sections which include a boiler, a turbine and a generator. The boiler is filled with water and the fuels are burnt to boil the water to produce steam. The steam drives the turbine, which rotates and in turn drives the generator. As the generator rotates, electrical energy is produced.

[8]

2 Based on the paragraph from question 1, complete these sentences with the correct forms of energy.

The _____ energy of the fuels is converted to _____ energy which boils the water. This energy in the steam is further changed to _____ energy, thus turning the turbines. This energy is again changed into _____ energy by the generator.

[4]

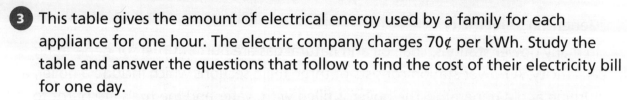

3 This table gives the amount of electrical energy used by a family for each appliance for one hour. The electric company charges 70¢ per kWh. Study the table and answer the questions that follow to find the cost of their electricity bill for one day.

Electrical appliance	Consumption (kW) per hour
Air conditioning	3·5
Water heater	2·2
100 W bulbs	0·1
Computer	0·8
Iron	1·4
Refrigerator	0·6

Cost

a) Air conditioner for 6 hours   = 6 × 3·5 × 70¢   = _____

b) Water heater for 3 hours   = 3 × 2·2 × 70¢   = _____

c) 6 light bulbs, each for 4 hours   =   = _____

d) Computer for 8 hours   =   = _____

e) Iron for 1½ hours   =   = _____

f) Refrigerator 24 hours   =   = _____

Total cost for one day   = _____

g) The number of kWh of electricity usage is adjusted for ALL customers. If that adjustment were not made, what would be the electricity bill for only these appliances for this family for a 30-day month?

Do your calculations in this box.

_____ × 30

= _____

[8]

11.7   Nuclear energy

1 Nuclear energy is released in nuclear fusion and nuclear _____. [1]

2 Decide whether the following statements are TRUE or FALSE.

a) Nuclear energy is produced in power plants as a result of nuclear fission.

_____

b) When uranium atoms are split, thermal energy is released. _____

c) A disadvantage of splitting uranium is that too little energy is produced.

_____

d) Animals but not plants are affected by nuclear energy pollution. _____ [4]

3 Circle the answer that describes what happens to uranium atoms at a nuclear power plant:

a) They combine to give off heat energy.

b) They burn to give off heat energy.

c) They burn to combine.

d) They split to become smaller atoms. [1]

4 Identify the disadvantage of using nuclear energy:

a) Radioactive wastes are produced.

b) Air pollution occurs.

c) Fission produces small amounts of energy.

d) Fusion produces too much energy. [2]

5 In fusion small atoms combine to form larger ones but in nuclear fission

_____

_____ . [1]

11.8 Non-renewable energy sources

1 From the sources of energy shown here, circle the non-renewable ones.

[5]

2 Fossil fuels are _____ .

[1]

3 Give TWO disadvantages of fossil fuels.

a) _____

b) _____

[2]

For questions 4–6, circle the correct answer.

4 A non-renewable resource is one that is:

a) non-replaceable

b) replaced slower than it is used

c) found deep in the Earth's crust

d) not possible to exhaust.

5 What is gasoline produced from?

a) Natural gas   **b)** Coal   **c)** Biomass   **d)** Petroleum

6 Which of these energy sources is non-renewable?

a) Solar   **b)** Wind   **c)** Natural gas   **d)** Biomass

[3]

11.9 Renewable energy sources

For questions 1–3, circle the correct answer.

1 Some sources of energy are renewable because they

   a) can be naturally replenished within a short period of time

   b) are clean and free to use

   c) can change easily from one form to another

   d) are not factors of pollution.

   [1]

2 Which of these is a renewable resource of energy?

   a) Geothermal   b) Solar   c) Wind   d) All of these

   [1]

3 Renewable resources are:

   a) no cleaner than non-renewable resources

   b) limited by cost, but not supply

   c) often less abundant than non-renewable resources

   d) all of these.

   [1]

4 Choose the answer which matches each source of energy. Put A, B, C, D, E or F in the boxes provided in the table on the right.

A	Fossil fuel
B	Coal
C	Electricity
D	Solar
E	Natural gas
F	Sun

	Is a renewable source of energy
	Can be produced from chemical energy
	Provides a great deal of energy
	Is the original source of energy
	Is found in dangerous environments
	Is transported in pipelines

[6]

11.10 Biofuels

1 Whereas many forms of energy are made from non-living matter, biofuels are made from _____ materials.

[1]

2 The primary energy source for animals and plants is:

a) water **b)** fertilizer **c)** sunlight **d)** nutrients in the soil.

[1]

3 Which of these is an example of biofuel?

a) Trees **b)** Wind **c)** Water **d)** Soil

[2]

4 Choose TRUE or FALSE for each of these statements.

a) Biofuel is fuel from non-fossilized organic matter. _____

b) Both petroleum and biofuels are from the same source. _____

c) The energy stored by plants is used as biofuel. _____

d) Many plants contain oil in their seeds. _____

e) Sunflower oil from the grocery store cannot be used as biofuel. _____

[5]

5 Give TWO reasons for using biofuel as an alternative source of energy.

a) _____

_____

_____

b) _____

_____

_____

[2]

11.11   Transforming energy

1 Here are some electrical appliances. Study each one and complete the table to explain what form of energy each appliance starts with and what it converts this energy into.

	APPLIANCE	STARTING ENERGY	FINISHING ENERGY FORMS
A			
B			
C			
D			
E			

[5]

2 Name FOUR items which have potential energy that is NOT electrical, and name the type of potential energy each does have.

a) _____ – _____

b) _____ – _____

c) _____ – _____

d) _____ – _____

[4]

3 Use linking lines to match each object with the correct energy outputs.

a)

| Light |
| Heat |
| Sound |
| Movement |

b)

| Sound |
| Light |
| Movement |
| Heat |

c)

| Light |
| Heat |
| Sound |
| Movement |

d)

| Sound |
| Light |
| Movement |
| Heat |

e)

| Light |
| Heat |
| Sound |
| Movement |

f)

| Sound |
| Light |
| Movement |
| Heat |

[6]

11.12 Law of conservation of energy

1 What does the law of conservation of energy state? _____

_____

[1]

2 According to the law of conservation of energy, say whether the following are TRUE or FALSE

a) There is no increase in the amount of energy in the universe. _____

b) The total energy before a reaction is always less than the total energy after a reaction. _____

c) The amount of energy both before and after a change remains constant.

_____

d) When a candle burns the energy produced is the same as its potential energy.

_____

e) The energy produced during sleep is less than that produced during high jumping.

_____

[5]

3 a) The energy input and useful energy of each of these bulbs is given. Calculate the efficiency of each one.

Energy input	a) 100 J	b) 60 J	c) 75 J	d) 120 J
Useful energy	25 J	30 J	15 j	20 J
Efficiency				

[4]

b) Which bulb has the highest efficiency? _____

[1]

c) Which bulb has the lowest efficiency? _____

[1]

11.13   Sankey diagrams

1 What does a Sankey diagram show? _____

_____

[1]

2 An energy-saving bulb is shown here.

Of the energy it produces, only 60% is transferred as light; the rest is converted to heat.

a) What percentage is wasted as heat? _____

[1]

A representation of the energy produced by the bulb has been started on the graph below. Each 2 mm represents 10%.

b) Complete the Sankey diagram to show how the energy is distributed.

[2]

c) Identify each separation of the Sankey diagram.

[2]

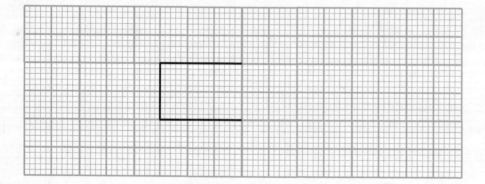

Study each Sankey diagram and fill in the blanks.

3 Ironing a sheet.

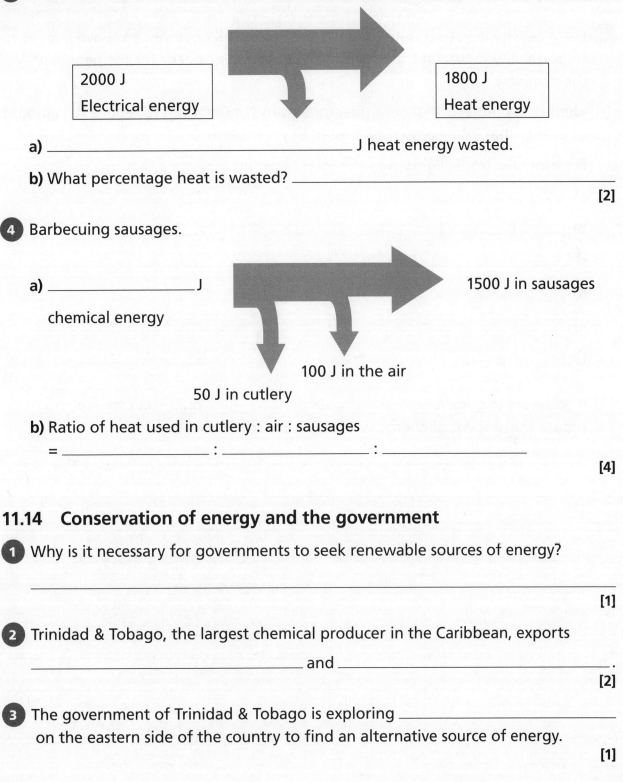

2000 J
Electrical energy

1800 J
Heat energy

a) _____ J heat energy wasted.

b) What percentage heat is wasted? _____

[2]

4 Barbecuing sausages.

a) _____ J

chemical energy

1500 J in sausages

100 J in the air

50 J in cutlery

b) Ratio of heat used in cutlery : air : sausages

= _____ : _____ : _____

[4]

11.14 Conservation of energy and the government

1 Why is it necessary for governments to seek renewable sources of energy?

_____

[1]

2 Trinidad & Tobago, the largest chemical producer in the Caribbean, exports

_____ and _____.

[2]

3 The government of Trinidad & Tobago is exploring _____
on the eastern side of the country to find an alternative source of energy.

[1]

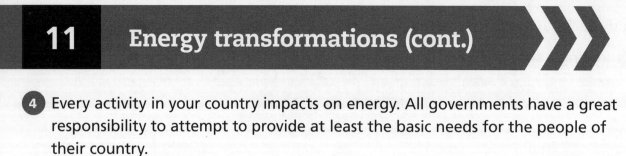

4 Every activity in your country impacts on energy. All governments have a great responsibility to attempt to provide at least the basic needs for the people of their country.

Identify SIX projects that your government has undertaken to reduce the amount of energy that is being used or wasted in your country.

For example, traffic lights are now solar powered.

a) _____

b) _____

c) _____

d) _____

e) _____

f) _____

[6]

5 If you were in government identify SIX projects you would want to implement to reduce the amount of energy wasted in your country.

_____

_____

_____

_____

_____

_____

_____

_____

_____

_____

_____

_____

[6]

11.15 Conservation of energy and the individual

1 Everyone can do a little to conserve energy. Below is a crossword puzzle. Use the clues on conserving energy to complete the puzzle.

Across	**Down**
1. _____ full loads in machine	1. _____ warm clothes when it is cold
4. _____ using 150 watt bulbs	2. _____ clothes outside to dry
8. _____ a garden	3. _____ smaller cars
11. _____ paper and plastic	5. _____ outdoors instead of watch TV for recreation
13. _____ tap while brushing your teeth	6. _____ appliances when on vacation
15. _____ a bike instead of driving	7. _____ kettle on gas
16. _____ curtains when it is hot	9. Close a _____ tap
17. _____ on both sides of paper	10. _____ showers instead of baths
18. _____ to energy saving bulbs	12. _____ off TV when no one is watching
	14. _____ off lights in an empty room

[10]

11 **Energy transformations (cont.)**

2 It is common to see logos with the words: REDUCE, REUSE, RECYCLE.

Create your own logo using these words. You may add a few more words to it, but keep it simple.

[5]